WHY I STOPPED DRINKING

And Why You Will Too

TABLE OF CONTENTS

MY STORY

It was a freezing cold day in March, 2003. I was 16 years old and working at a grocery store. I knew that my good friend Taylor was coming into town, so I asked one of my co-workers, who was of legal age, to buy a 60-ounce bottle of Jack Daniels for me. I thought it would be fun to party with Taylor and get wasted.

My co-worker bought the bottle and gave it to me, and I stuffed it in my backpack so my dad wouldn't see it when he picked me up from work. Then I went home, packed my hockey bag, and went to go play hockey.

Taylor came to my game, and afterwards he came back to my parents' house. We drank a few beers and then went and met my friend Cory and walked with him to the house of his girlfriend, Samantha. We went into her basement, opened the 60-ounce bottle of Jack Daniel's, and started drinking.

There were four of us who were drinking: Taylor, David, Michael, and me. We passed around the 60-ounce bottle of Jack Daniels until it was finished—in less than one hour.

We were so drunk that we became very loud and barely able to walk. And then Taylor went upstairs and drank an additional bottle of wine with Samantha's sister. Cory got mad because we were being loud and because he wanted to be alone with Samantha, so he kicked the four of us out.

It was minus 18 degrees Celsius that night.

We were so drunk that we hardly knew what was going on. As we walked down the street, Michael kicked a store window and alarms started to go off. We heard police sirens and ran and we got separated. I was with Taylor, and I said, "Why don't we go back to my parents' house. I have some weed there that we can smoke."

About half of the way back to my parents' house, Taylor started to pass out. I began carrying him, and he told me to leave him, and he tried to punch me in the face. I said, no, again and again, but when I realized that he couldn't keep going, I left to go and get help.

I walked back to my parents' house and blacked out.

The next day I woke up with my sister telling me that Taylor's parents were on the phone, and a boy was found outside passed out in the freezing cold and he was on the news.

Then Taylor's parents called and I spoke with his father, Joseph, who told me that Taylor was found, his body was frozen, and the doctor said that they were going to cut off his arms from the elbows down, and they were going to cut off his legs from his knees down.

I started to cry. I hung up the phone, called the police, and told them that it was all my fault.

The police officer assured me that it was not my fault and told me to come into the police station to testify. I went into the police station the next day. I explained how we drank a 60-

ounce bottle of Jack Daniel's in one hour on the night that Taylor nearly froze to death. I cried my eyes out as I told the story to the police as my dad sat beside me. I have never felt more anguished.

Then I went to Sunnybrook Hospital, where Taylor had been taken. When I first saw him, his arms and legs were completely black, and one doctor had said it would be best to cut off his arms from the elbows down and his legs from the knees down.

Fortunately, there was another doctor who said to wait.

Taylor ended up having an incredibly tough battle to recovery, and he eventually had to have his big toe amputated. He has since recovered, but he still feels the effects from the severe frostbite and has moved to a foreign country because he cannot bear the freezing cold temperatures in Canada.

I stopped drinking.

I didn't drink for several months. But then once Taylor had recovered, and I knew that he was drinking again, I started drinking again too.

In the next decade and a half I spent tens of thousands of dollars on alcohol and made more bad, potentially life-altering mistakes.

And then, at last, I stopped drinking, this time for good.

This book is the story of how I got there.

Alcohol Is an Addiction

A study published in Science Translational Medicine found that people who drink have higher spikes in endorphins. Endorphins are responsible for the feelings of pleasure and reward in the brain, which enables people to temporarily feel good while drinking alcohol, and because this feeling is temporary, people become addicted to alcohol.[1] Alcohol is the third most addictive drug in the world, next to cocaine and heroin.[2]

I was already drinking heavily regularly when I was in high school, and I was getting into trouble regularly because of it. So were my friends.

When I was 16, I was at a party super drunk after drinking two large bottles of Lucky Lager. I saw my friend Cory taking a piss on his neighbour's lawn. A man came out of his house, grabbed Cory by the throat and threw him down the hill, and he rolled naked with his pants down. I saw this and grabbed my bottle and threw it through the man's window. Then I ducked into the bushes with Cory and we got out of there.

We started breaking into cars to look for anything that we could steal, because we didn't have jobs at the time, and so we didn't have money, and we were drunk, and we wanted to drink more. All of a sudden, I saw a Suburban roll up. Two huge police officers got out with a German shepherd.

I started running between them and they clotheslined me. Then they started punching me in the kidney until I screamed "That's enough!" and gave in.

---

[1] Amanda L. Chan, "Why Alcohol Is So Addictive," *Huffingtonpost.ca,* January 12, 2013. https://www.huffingtonpost.ca/entry/alcohol-addictive-endorphins-_n_1202406.

[2] Editorial Staff, "What Is the Most Addictive Drug? Here Are the Top 5," American Addiction Centers, March 23, 2020. https://americanaddictioncenters.org/adult-addiction-treatment-programs/most-addictive.

This was at 4 in the morning.

The police did not know that I threw a beer bottle through a house window. They arrested me for breaking into cars. I was handcuffed and taken home to my parents and I had to later appear in court.

The charges were dropped because I didn't actually steal anything—but I did throw a bottle through a window, and someone could have been seriously injured… and that man had to pay for that window.

***

When I was 17, I was at a bar with a few of my friends and one of them decided to steal a Budweiser umbrella. He grabbed it but the bartender noticed that he was stealing it. He ran with the umbrella. I foolishly jumped on the back of his car and held on for dear life as he put the pedal to the medal. Then after a few hundred metres he turned sharply and I fell off of the car.

Luckily, I had a lot of experience with snowboarding and skateboarding and I knew to roll and how to fall. I broke my fall with my shoulder but still hit my head and got a concussion. I was rushed to hospital and had a bump on my head that lasted for weeks. I was lucky I didn't get permanent brain damage—or die.

***

When I was 19, for my ex-girlfriend's 19th birthday, I joined four girls at a bar in Barrie, Ontario. We were all dancing and drinking a lot. At the end of the night, I was too drunk to drive, but I drove anyways, with the four girls as my passengers.

5

As I was driving home, all of a sudden it became very foggy and I lost control of the car and spun into a ditch. I was thankful that no one was injured, but I was worried and didn't know what to do.

After 10 minutes or so, a man with a truck came out of nowhere and parked his truck close to where my car was in the ditch. He walked toward me and asked if I had been drinking.

One of the girls, Tiffany, said, "No, he has not been drinking." The man came right up to my face and asked me if I was drinking.

"No," I lied.

He went back to his truck, got his winch, and pulled my car out of the ditch.

I was stupid, and I was lucky. I was never caught for drinking and driving. But I have known several people who have been arrested and charged for being reckless and driving under the influence of alcohol and have gotten their car impounded. A few of them spent time in jail. They had to pay lawyers, their driver's licence was suspended, their car insurance skyrocketed, and they now have a criminal record.

Drinking and Driving

About 28 percent of all traffic fatalities involve alcohol.[3] When you drive under the influence of alcohol, you are not only putting yourself in danger, you are also putting

---

[3] National Highway Traffic Safety Administration, "Traffic Safety Facts 2016 data: alcohol-impaired driving," US Department of Transportation, October 2017. https://crashstats.nhtsa.dot.gov/Api/Public/ViewPublication/812450.

others at risk as well. Drinking and driving is a fatal mistake that thousands of people make each year, and it happens because alcohol leads to bad decisions.[4]

When I was 21 years old, I was living at my parents' house and working at a factory. After saving up a few paychecks, I decided to go to the liquor store and stock up my parents' bar. I loaded up two carts with liquor and spent over $1,000. And then I immediately invited a few of my friends over.

We started taking shots of alcohol and ended up having at least 18 drinks in a short period of time.

Cory said we should drive to the casino. I drove to Cory's mom's house. She said he couldn't take her car because he was too drunk to drive. He kept complaining until I made a terrible decision: I drove us to the casino nearly blackout drunk.

I barely remember being at the casino. We were only there for a short time. Then we left and I had to drive home—my friends were passed out. As I drove, I started falling asleep. I kept slapping myself in the face as hard as I could just to stay awake. Even with that, I fell asleep momentarily and saw myself in the middle of the highway for a split second.

Then luckily, I woke up.

We were so fortunate that no one was killed that night.

***

---

4 "Statistics," MADD Canada, accessed June 13, 2020.
https://madd.ca/pages/impaired-driving/overview/statistics/

In early 2011, I was in Las Vegas with some good friends. One friend, named Max, took us all out for dinner to thank us for a favour. Over the course of the evening, Max drank several beers and several bottles of Soju. And at the end of the night, when everyone was leaving the restaurant and saying goodbye, he could barely walk. We left the restaurant, and he said to everyone that he was going to drive home.

Max had the keys to his Porsche in his hand, and he attempted to put them in his car. I decided that it was far too dangerous for Max to drive. I remembered the other things that had happened in my life. I got in front of him and said, "No, you are not driving."

He threatened me for a minute. Then he said, "You're probably right," and called a cab.

Alcohol Is Poison

According to a comprehensive study by *The Lancet Psychiatry*, alcohol kills approximately three million people each year, and alcohol use is a leading risk factor for disease burden worldwide. Alcohol accounts for nearly 10% of global deaths among populations aged 15 to 49.

The study concluded that the safest amount of alcohol to consume is none.[5]

According to the World Health Organization's guide for monitoring alcohol consumption and related harm, there are at least 61 illnesses, injuries, or causes of death generated by alcohol consumption.

---

[5] L. Degenhardt et al., "The global burden of disease attributable to alcohol and drug use in 195 countries and territories, 1990–2016: A systematic analysis for the Global Burden of Disease Study 2016," *Lancet Psychiatry*, 5(12): 987–1012. https://www.thelancet.com/journals/lancet/article/PIIS0140-6736(18)31310-2/fulltext

In October 2006, my friend Michael and I drove to St. Catharines from Aurora, Ontario. Cory was having a house party, and when we got there, he was already drunk. We brought a 40-ounce bottle of Southern Comfort. When Cory saw they bottle, he grabbed it and chugged almost the entire bottle all at once.

I knew immediately that he would get alcohol poisoning because I had a lot of experience partying and being around people who drink. Sure enough, about an hour after he chugged the liquor, he passed out and was not responding. I was thinking about calling an ambulance because I knew that he had to have his stomach pumped.

Instead, I did something that I shouldn't have done: I put my fingers down in his throat and made him vomit.

He ended up puking a lot, and he turned out to be alright. But he could have choked, he could have bitten my fingers off… and he also could have died from alcohol poisoning.

***

Cory and Taylor weren't my only friends who drank too much. One snowy December evening, I was in Boston Massachusetts, and I went out for drinks with a couple of friends. That night we were drinking heavily, and my friend Kevin got so drunk that we had to call an ambulance and he had to be rushed to hospital to have his stomach pumped because he had alcohol poisoning.

He recovered… but he could have died.

***

In 2009, I was at a New Year's Eve party in Aurora, Ontario. I had a few beers, and I noticed that Michael, who was with me on the night that Taylor nearly died, had been drinking a lot at the party and was nowhere to be seen. I went with my intuition and went outside and looked out into the forest and saw Michael passed out in the grass—on a winter night, in Canada.

I ran up to him and woke him up. He was not making sense. I carried him back to the house and he said that he was going to walk home. So I walked with him.

He tried to fight me as he was stumbling. Then he told me to leave him. I remembered what happened to Taylor back in 2003. I said "No." And I continued to walk with him all the way back to his parents' house.

When we got back to his parents' house, he was acting like a child, and he tried to fight me and to fight his parents because he was so drunk and out of control.

Imagine if I hadn't found him. Imagine if I had left him when he told me to.

The Negative Effects of Alcohol on Your Body

People who regularly drink alcohol increase their risk of experiencing liver damage, heart damage, lung infections, thinning bones, shrinking brain, malnutrition, infertility, complications of diabetes, and erectile dysfunction.

Drinking alcohol decreases oxygen and blood flow to the genitals. Because alcohol dehydrates your body, it can also lower your desire for sex and prevent sex hormone production.[6] Heavy drinking leads to vaginal dryness and prevents male erections.[7] According to a study conducted at the University of Washington, alcohol affects your brain and your penis. The study confirmed that drunk men were not able to have an erection as fast as sober men.[8]

Alcohol also contains acid and stains tooth enamel. Alcoholics are three times as likely to experience permanent tooth loss. Alcohol use increases the probability of getting gum diseases, tooth decay, and mouth sores—as well as oral cancer.[9]

Alcohol Increases Your Risk of Cancer

A Canadian federally funded study examining the introduction of cancer warning labels on containers was shut down following industry interference, despite the fact that the World Health Organization classified alcohol as a class one carcinogen thirty years ago.[10] Alcoholic

---

6 A. Pietrangelo and K. Holland, "23 Effects of Alcohol on Your Body," *Healthline,* September 28, 2018. https://www.healthline.com/health/alcohol/effects-on-body

7 American Addiction Centers Editorial Staff, "Is Alcohol Wreaking Havoc on Your Sexual Performance?" *DrugAbuse.com,* July 25, 2019. https://drugabuse.com/is-alcohol-wreaking-havoc-on-your-sexual-performance/

8 Chris Iliades and Farrokh Sohrabi, "Why Boozing Can Be Bad for Your Sex Life," *Everyday Health,* January 4, 2012. https://www.everydayhealth.com/erectile-dysfunction/why-boozing-can-be-bad-for-your-sex-life.aspx

9 Elea Carey, "What Does Alcohol Do to Your Teeth?" *Healthline,* September 29, 2018. https://www.healthline.com/health/dental-and-oral-health/what-does-alcohol-do-to-your-teeth

10 Tim Stockwell, Robert Solomon, Paula O'Brien, Kate Vallance, and Eric Hobin, "Cancer Warning Labels on Alcohol Containers: A Consumer's Right to Know, a Government's Responsibility to Inform, and an Industry's Power to Thwart," *Journal of Studies on Alcohol and Drugs,* 81(2): 284–292. https://www.jsad.com/doi/full/10.15288/jsad.2020.81.284#

beverages are in the same category as second-hand tobacco smoke and processed meat.[11]

According to a study, "Light Alcohol Drinking and Cancer: A Meta-Analysis," there is strong evidence that moderate to heavy alcohol consumption increases the probability of getting diseases such as cancer of the colorectum, breast, larynx, liver, esophagus, oral cavity, and pharynx.

The study further concluded light drinking increased the probability of oral cancer as well as female breast cancer.[12] Alcohol consumption can also lead to birth defects in babies.

In 2014, I was at my friend Stefan's cottage with a bunch of people and I drank way too much. A bunch of us were in the kitchen and one of us pulled out a bag of cocaine. I did a line.

It was the first time in a long time that I had done cocaine. I was already drunk and my heart was racing. I decided to go down to Stefan's dock and go swimming in the lake late at night, by myself.

I fell asleep underwater.

I remember my friend Alex came down to the dock and yelled "Kyle!" and I woke up just in time. If Alex had not come at that time, I most likely would have drowned.

***

---

[11] American Cancer Society, "Known and Probable Human Carcinogens," *Cancer.org*, August 14, 2019. https://www.cancer.org/cancer/cancer-causes/general-info/known-and-probable-human-carcinogens.html

[12] V. Bagnardi et al., "Light alcohol drinking and cancer: a meta-analysis," *Annals of Oncology* 24(2): 301–308. https://doi.org/10.1093/annonc/mds337

When I lived in the Philippines, I co-founded a mobile gaming company, Jungle Friend Studios. One of my best friends, Max, took in a man who was close to becoming homeless. This man's name was Brody. He was an alcoholic and a cocaine addict who partied out of control.

When he was working at Jungle Friend Studios, he would go out for days and party, and I would have to chase after him. He was doing lots of drugs, and he constantly broke the momentum and focus of the company. Eventually, Max and I decided to fire him.

After he was fired, he turned to dealing drugs. I did not hear from him for a long time after that. The last time that I spoke with Brody, he was in prison in the Philippines because he got caught with drugs.

The Philippines is one of the worst places in the world to get caught with drugs. It has terrible overcrowded prisons in horrific conditions, and it gives some of the harshest sentences in the world for drug-related crimes.[13]

Early Exposure to Alcohol Increases the Risk of Drug Addiction

91% of cocaine users between 18 and 49 years old tried alcohol before cocaine. Of this group, 5.1% mixed both alcohol and cocaine together.[14]

---

[13] American Addiction Centers Editorial Staff, "The 20 Countries with the Harshest Drug Laws in the World," *DrugAbuse.com*, August 18, 2020.
https://drugabuse.com/the-20-countries-with-the-harshest-drug-laws-in-the-world/

[14] Edmund A. Griffin Jr. et al., "Prior alcohol use enhances vulnerability to compulsive cocaine self-administration by promoting degradation of HDAC4 and HDAC5," *Science Advances* 3(11).
https://advances.sciencemag.org/content/3/11/e1701682

A study conducted on how alcohol increases a person's vulnerability to addiction to cocaine revealed that most people who use an illicit drug do not develop an addiction to it. However, consuming alcohol can increase the probability of that person developing an addiction.

Researchers separated two groups of rats into different cages. One group was issued water for two hours before starting to use cocaine, and the other received alcohol before cocaine. The rats in the group with the alcohol in their cage used and abused the cocaine more frequently, even when they had a negative shock consequence.[15]

Birth Defects from Alcohol

Women who drink when they are pregnant put their unborn child at risk of fetal alcohol syndrome, which can lead to learning and physical development abnormalities, increased emotional problems, long-term health issues, and learning difficulties.

Why would you want to risk becoming addicted to something that can cripple or deform an unborn child?[16]

One of my best friends in the Philippines, Tyler, was a very good-looking man who could get almost any woman that he

[15] "VIDEO: How Alcohol Influences Cocaine Addiction," Columbia University Irving Medical Center, November 3, 2017.
https://www.cuimc.columbia.edu/news/video-how-alcohol-influences-cocaine-addiction; B.F Grant et al., "Epidemiology of *DSM-5* drug use disorder: Results from the National Epidemiologic Survey on Alcohol and Related Conditions–III," *JAMA Psychiatry* 73: 39–47.

[16] "Fetal Alcohol Effects," *AboutBirthDefects.org*, accessed June 14, 2020.
http://www.aboutbirthdefects.org/fetal-alcohol-effects/

wanted. One night we went to a club and he met a woman named Rena. He danced with her and ended up going home with her that night, and she asked him to take off his condom. He made a bad decision and took off his condom and had sex with her unprotected.

A few days later he asked me what I would do if I woke up with a rash all over my groin. I said I would go to the doctor. He started crying saying that it had happened to him.

He ended up being diagnosed with herpes, a disease that is not yet curable. He will have to live with that for the rest of his life because of one bad decision made while drinking alcohol.

Sexual Assault and STIs

An abundance of studies have shown a strong correlation between alcohol consumption and sexually transmitted infections (STIs). Alcohol gives people who drink it a temporary boost in confidence and can lead them to riskier decisions that are not thought out. A person can black out and end up going home with someone they would not have if they were not drinking.

Does this sound like an overstatement? Here are some statistics: "26 percent of males and nearly 36 percent of females failed to use a condom during sex with someone they met on spring break—and alcohol use played a role in this behaviour." And "49 percent of men and 38 percent of women reported having sex as the direct result of drinking."[17]

---

[17] Jasmine Bittar, "Alcohol and STDs," *Alcohol Rehab Guide*, November 5, 2019. https://www.alcoholrehabguide.org/resources/medical-conditions/alcohol-and-stds/

To make matters worse, approximately 50 percent of all sexual assaults that occur involve the assaulter, the victim, or both being under the influence of alcohol.[18]

Alcohol-Related Death

The Global Burden of Disease reported alcohol-related deaths and the extent of social and other disability due to alcohol. It was estimated that alcohol is the leading cause of disability for men in developed countries. Eight global regions were examined and it was reported that alcohol was responsible for 636,800 deaths, 14.6 million years of lost life, and 32.3 million "disability adjusted" years of lost life in 1990.[19]

And the deaths caused by alcohol are on the rise. In 2012, alcohol was reportedly responsible for 3.3 million deaths, an increase of over 500% in deaths in less than 25 years.[20]

I used to know a man who called himself "Chase White, shine so bright." We used to hang out all the time. I went to Montréal with him on a business trip. One night when I was not with him, he was doing cocaine and drank 16 shots of tequila, and then he decided to drive.

---

[18] Antonia Abbey, Tina Zawacki, Philip O. Buck, A. Monique Clinton, and Pam McAuslan, "Sexual Assault and Alcohol Consumption: What Do We Know about Their Relationship and What Types of Research are Still Needed?" *Aggression and Violent Behavior* 9(3): 271–303.
https://www.ncbi.nlm.nih.gov/pmc/articles/PMC4616254/

[19] World Health Organization, *International Guide for Monitoring Alcohol Consumption and Related Harm*, 2000.

[20] "Alcohol," World Health Organisation, accessed June 14, 2020.
https://www.who.int/substance_abuse/facts/alcohol/en/

He told me the next day how lucky he was to be alive... because he drove on the wrong side of a highway.

After he told me this, I cut back my drinking drastically, and I eventually stopped hanging out with him altogether because he was a bad influence on me.

***

I was in Utah visiting one of my best friends and a mutual friend was having a party. Most of the people at the party were wasted, as usual.

We all started playing Yahtzee and after a few rolls I rolled a Yahtzee. I took a shot of whiskey that was on the table and put the bottle in front of the only sober person at sitting at the table, my good friend CH.

CH scolded me, saying that he doesn't drink and that he's been to rehab for alcohol and cocaine addiction and he will never drink or do drugs again.

I began looking around at everyone at the party and saw them being obnoxious, not making any sense—and I started asking myself, why am I drinking?

I ended up going back to my friend's house that night and woke up hung over the next morning.

Quitting Is Not Easy

Alcohol is highly addictive. Quitting alcohol is not easy—and it can be life threatening for heavy drinkers.

There two types of alcohol withdrawal. One is moderate alcohol withdrawal, which typically happens after a few hours or several days after a person's last drink. These symptoms include fever, muscle pains, irregular heartbeat, fatigue, shakiness, and difficulty sleeping.

The second and most severe form of alcohol withdrawal is called delirium tremens. Delirium tremens causes fatigue, hallucinations, fear, excitement, irritability, body tremors, and seizures.[21]

On October 28, 2018, I met up with a few of my good friends. Cory was back in town and we all had not seen each other in five years.

That night I travelled from Niagara Falls to Toronto. Cory and I met up at the hotel and later went out drinking and we met up with everyone else. We had a lot of drinks. We did shots together. I don't even remember leaving the bar.

A few hours later, Cory and Adam came into my hotel room, and they found me in the bathtub passed out in the water. I have no idea how I got there. Adam pulled me out of the bathtub.

The next night I went to a party with people I wanted to connect with. I was very hung over. I did not make a great first impression with them, and you only get one chance to make a first impression.

But at least I was still alive.

---

[21] Ann Pietrangelo, "Night Sweats and Alcohol," *Healthline*, September 29, 2018. https://www.healthline.com/health/night-sweats-and-alcohol

Who Are You Hanging Out With?

I realized that when I was hanging out with these groups of people, we were constantly making bad decisions—and they were all alcoholics, like me. I had tried many times to quit drinking alcohol, but I never realized the importance of a person's inner circle. I would continue to get drunk and go back to hanging out with the same groups of drinkers. Whenever I would say that I'm not drinking anymore, someone would say "You've changed," or "Come on, you pussy," or "Be a man, you can't handle your alcohol?" I finally learned that I shouldn't take it personally: when they say that, they are showing a reflection of the pain and insecurity inside of themselves. They are being like the crabs in a bucket that are trying to pull any crab that tries to escape back in.

According to motivational speaker Jim Rohn, we are the average of the five people we spend the most time with… so choose them wisely. If the people you're hanging out with are constantly drinking and encouraging you to make bad decisions, then it might be time to pick a new group of friends.

Even after all of these experiences, even after I became a vegan, even after I had published two books, I still had not stopped drinking. And it kept costing me opportunities. In the summer of 2019, after I published my first book, *The Christian Bubble*, I made plans to go from Cincinnati to Omaha to do my best to give a copy of my book to the oracle of Omaha, Warren Buffett. My plan was to deliver the book to Buffett's doorstep.

I had already messaged his son Peter Buffett, on Facebook and I told him that I was going to Omaha for the weekend.

But I got drunk at a party and misplaced my keys. Which meant I had to cancel my flight, which cost me $100, as well as my Airbnb... and the opportunity to give my book to Warren Buffett.

Habits

Because I followed my heart and intuition and became a human and animal rights activist and then an author, I learned the importance of mindset. I met my friend Pierluigi through watching and studying videos on producing audiobooks. Pierluigi told me that mindset was a key to success. He told me to follow Bob Proctor and watch his videos. Proctor's videos have improved my mindset tremendously.

It turns out that Bob Proctor also had a drinking problem. He was going to bars and spending lots of his money. And one day it occurred to him that the people he saw in the bars were all bums. Then he made the connection that if he was in the bars that he must be a bum too.

Proctor immediately put his drink down and made the decision to never go back to the bars—and he never did. Proctor talks about drinking as a bad habit: an idea that has been planted inside of your subconscious mind that you act on without giving any conscious thought. And, Proctor, says, if you don't replace a bad habit with a good habit, you'll automatically create another bad habit.[22]

---

[22] Abundance Mentality, *All You Need Is Six Minutes ~Bob Proctor*, YouTube video, July 8, 2017. https://www.youtube.com/watch?v=LF-wLJvTnng

So it's important to develop good habits: exercise, learning new skills or instruments, learning new languages, helping out in your community… the possibilities for doing good in the world are limitless.

I should have noticed sooner what kind of company I was in as a heavy drinker. In my later 20s I had a few alcoholic roommates in their late 40s who had failed marriages and relationships. I saw how they had turned to alcohol as a way to escape, and I also saw how the alcohol had ruined their families, their relationships, and their whole lives.

But when I lived with Uncle Bobby, it was a wake-up call that I will never forget.

I was living in Windsor, Ontario. I moved in to live with a man in his late 40s. He seemed like a good person when he was sober, when I first moved in with him, but the first weekend I noticed that he drank a lot. He got drunk to the point where he would run around saying "Bob's your uncle," not making any sense, which is why I call him "Uncle Bobby."

When the Covid-19 pandemic happened, Uncle Bobby was laid off. This led him to drinking alcohol nearly every day. I would go to the fridge and see it stocked with beer and I knew that Uncle Bobby would be getting hammered for no reason. He would wake up at 10 AM and start drinking beers until he was loud and obnoxious.

This became a daily habit. The more he drank, the more I began to hate alcohol and its smell. And Uncle Bobby was constantly drunk.

One night he had a few prostitutes over, and was asking me if

I wanted to have sex with one of them. I believe that it is wrong for a lot of reasons, so I said no.

Then, two nights later, he had an older lady over, and she passed out on the couch because she was drunk. I came out of my room at 3AM, and saw him touching her while she was passed out. I realized what was happening and started talking loudly and distracting him, while channeling my energy for her to wake up. She woke up and immediately asked me for a drive home.

I drove her home, and when I got back, Uncle Bobby was there, and I was telling him how stupid it was for him to have her over when she was that drunk. He started telling me that he will fuck anything that walks. He said that he has had a bunch of STDs. And then he said that he gave HPV to his daughter.[23]

He changed the tone of his voice and said that she got HPV from a toilet seat. But I looked into his eyes and read him. I went and checked: is it possible to get HPV from a toilet seat? No, it is not.[24]

I knew that Uncle Bobby had sex with his daughter. And I knew I had to get out of there immediately. He had also been watching tons of murder mysteries and weird conspiracy theory videos. He was not a safe person to be near.

While Uncle Bobby was passed out on the couch, I went with

---

[23] Amber Erickson Gabbey, "Everything you Need to Know About Human Papillomavirus Infection," *Healthline*, February 25, 2020.
https://www.healthline.com/health/human-papillomavirus-infection

[24] Lisa Fayed, "Can You Get the HPV Virus From a Public Toilet Seat?" *Verywell Health*, September 17, 2020. https://www.verywellhealth.com/hpv-and-toilet-seats-514137

my instincts: I pulled an all-nighter, packed all my things, and got in my car and drove to Montreal.

And I stopped drinking for good.

The Cost of Alcohol

The cost of alcohol adds up.

According to the Bureau of Labor Statistics, approximately 1% of Americans' gross annual income is spent on alcohol. That is about $565 per year, $5,650 in 10 years, or $28,250 over 50 years.[25]

Meanwhile, 40% of Americans can't come up with $400 for an unexpected expense.[26]

Why Waste Life?

The average life expectancy in the United States is 78.5 years. That is approximately 28,653 days, 688,117 hours or 4,095 weeks or life on planet earth. And none of these days are guaranteed because of the variance of dying before 78.5.

This means that if you are 35, you have approximately 2,270 weeks left.

Do you want to waste precious time on Planet Earth being drunk or hung over?

---

[25] Alaya Linton, "How Much Does Drinking Really Cost?" *The Balance Everyday*, August 24, 2018. https://www.thebalanceeveryday.com/what-lifetime-of-drinking-costs-4142309

[26] Annia Nova, "Many Americans who can't afford a $400 emergency blame debt," *CNBC*, July 20, 2019. https://www.cnbc.com/2019/07/20/heres-why-so-many-americans-cant-handle-a-400-unexpected-expense.html

I have wasted hundreds of days of my life being hung over and not productive. I could have been killed many times and there were many times of extreme danger caused by drinking.

I am so fortunate that I was born into privilege and did not end up dead or homeless from my poor decisions.

WHO ELSE?

I'm not the only person who nearly destroyed his life with alcohol. There are many others—some of them famous people you've heard of. Let me tell you about a few people whose lives were strongly affected by alcohol.

Cristiano Ronaldo

Most people know that Cristiano Ronaldo is an international football icon. He currently plays for Serie A club Juventus. He is the captain of the Portuguese national team. He also holds 145 footballing records, including most Champions League goals, most goals in all European competitions, and the first player to score in every minute of a game.

But Ronaldo's great success did not come easily for him.

His father was an alcoholic.

Cristiano Ronaldo's father, José Aveiro, was forced to go to war for Portugal in Angola and Mozambique. During the war the Portuguese soldiers ate rotting food and nearly starved in horrific conditions. A lot of the men were bedridden and ill with fevers, chills, and malaria. Because the soldiers did not have access to clean water, they would mostly drink Angolan beer.[27]

Aveiro returned home to Portugal after enduring thirteen months of hellish war conditions. During these times, it was tough to find a job, because the Portuguese military dictatorship used lots of money and resources on the war, so the economy was bad. So Aveiro went to local bars and pubs, where he would receive free drinks because he was a war veteran.

According to Maria Dolores, his wife, Aveiro was drunk all of the time, nearly every day. She also said that although he had never assaulted their kids, he had assaulted her.[28]

Aveiro eventually got a job as a gardener, and he later worked for Sant Antoni as a kit man. That was the team that his son, Ronaldo, played for. Ronaldo's teammates would poke fun at him and his father for working as a kitman. This just motivated Ronaldo to become the best player he could.

José Aveiro passed away in 2005 when he was 51, of liver failure from alcoholism, when Ronaldo was playing for Old Trafford. Ronaldo was only 20 years old. [29]

---

[27] Jon Boon, "Cristiano Ronaldo's alcoholic dad was a soldier who fought in Africa and died before seeing his son become a footballing superstar," *The Sun*, September 20, 2019. https://www.thesun.co.uk/sport/football/9943794/cristiano-ronaldo-alcoholic-dad/

[28] "The Story of Cristiano Ronaldo's Father, José Dinis Aveiro," Facts Ninja, accessed June 6, 2020. https://www.factsninja.com/the-story-of-cristiano-ronaldos-father-jose-dinis-aveiro.html

[29] Jon Boon, "Cristiano Ronaldo's alcoholic dad was a soldier who fought in Africa and died before seeing his son become a footballing superstar," *The Sun*, September 20, 2019. https://www.thesun.co.uk/sport/football/9943794/cristiano-ronaldo-alcoholic-dad/

In a 2019, Ronaldo was interviewed by Piers Morgan on ITV. When Piers Morgan asked him about his father and his alcoholism, Ronaldo said, "I really don't know my father 100%. He was a drunk person. I never spoke with him like a normal conversation. It was hard." Ronaldo continued, crying: "To be the number one and he don't see nothing, and he don't see to receive awards, to see what I became."[30]

Bradley Cooper

You've seen Bradley Cooper in many movies. He has won 56 awards and has received 193 nominations for his work during his career.[31] In 2018, Cooper directed *A Star Is Born* and played the rock star Jackson Maine, who ultimately destroys his career and his life with alcohol. In some ways, Maine is who Cooper could have been—if he hadn't stopped drinking.

Bradley Cooper was addicted to alcohol and drugs when he was 29.

In an interview with Barbara Walters, Cooper was asked about giving up drinking. He told Walters that if he hadn't given up drinking, "I would never been sitting here with you. No way, no chance." He explained: "I wouldn't have been able to have access to myself or other people or even been able to take in other people if I hadn't changed my life. No way.

---

[30]"Cristiano Ronaldo Meets Piers Morgan—Tuesday 14 Apr 9 pm," *ITV Hub*, accessed June 13, 2020. https://www.itv.com/hub/cristiano-ronaldo-meets-piers-morgan/2a7810a0001

[31] IMDb, "Bradley Cooper," accessed June 15, 2020. https://www.imdb.com/name/nm0177896/awards?ref_=nm_awd

And I never would have been able to have relationships that I do. I never would have been able to take care of my father the way I did when he was sick. So many things."[32]

As Cooper has said, "If you do work really hard and you're with supportive people then you can do things that you never even dreamed possible."[33] Cooper has now been sober for over 15 years. And he helped Brad Pitt to become sober as well.

Brad Pitt

You know who Brad Pitt is, of course: movie star, philanthropist, all-around sexy nice guy. And I'm sure you know he was married to Angelina Jolie. The couple share six children. But they got a divorce in September, 2016.

The spark of the breakup was when Pitt and Jolie, flying together on a private plane, got into a fight about Pitt's drinking habits. Pitt committed himself to alcoholics anonymous for a year and a half after Jolie filed for divorce.[34]

Pitt attributes his sobriety to his friendship with Bradley Cooper: "I got sober because of this guy," he says of Cooper, "and every day has been happier ever since."[35]

---

[32] ABC News, "Bradley Cooper on His Late Father and Deciding to Get Sober," accessed June 7, 2020. https://abcnews.go.com/Entertainment/video/bradley-cooper-late-father-deciding-sober-35833584

[33] TheEllenShow, *Bradley Cooper Wants to Reunite with Lady Gaga for a Special 'A Star Is Born' Event*, YouTube video, April 25, 2019.
https://www.youtube.com/watch?v=X4Vt39WTw08

[34] Ben Carlson, B. (2020). "Everyone Struggles," *A Wealth of Common Sense*, September 6, 2019. https://awealthofcommonsense.com/2019/09/everyone-struggles/

[35] Good Morning America, *Brad Pitt reveals how Bradley Cooper led him to sobriety*, video, January 10, 2020. https://www.goodmorningamerica.com/wellness/video/brad-pitt-reveals-bradley-cooper-led-sobriety-68191734.

Eminem

Marshall Bruce Mathers III, better known as Eminem, is an American rapper, record producer, actor and songwriter. Rolling stone ranked Eminem as 83rd on their top 100 greatest artists of all-time list. He has sold more than 172 million albums, making him one of the best-selling artists of all time. He also founded the Marshall Mathers Foundation dedicated to helping underprivileged, disadvantaged, and at-risk youth kids in Detroit and surrounding areas. [36]

Eminem has had tremendous success in his career, but he also struggled with drug and alcohol addiction. He was producing records and had a problem with alcohol and drugs that he kept secret.

And then he overdosed and nearly died.

As he recalled, "In 2007, I overdosed on pills, and I went into the hospital. I was close to 230 pounds. I'm not sure how I got so big, but I have ideas. The coating on the Vicodin and the Valium I'd been taking for years leaves a hole in your stomach, so to avoid a stomach ache, I was constantly eating—and eating badly."[37]

Eminem says that his kids—and seeing a rehab counsellor once a week—helped him to stay sober.[38]

---

[36] "Marshall Mathers Foundation," Eminem.com, accessed June 22, 2020. https://www.eminem.com/news/marshall-mathers-foundation

[37] Deborah Solomon, "The Real Marshall Mathers," *New York Times*, June 16, 2010. https://www.nytimes.com/2010/06/20/magazine/20fob-q4-t.html

[38] Deborah Solomon, "The Real Marshall Mathers," *New York Times*, June 16, 2010. https://www.nytimes.com/2010/06/20/magazine/20fob-q4-t.html

He also gives credit to relentless exercise. After he got out of rehab, he began to run: 8.5 miles on the treadmill before he went to work at the studio in the morning, and another 8.5 miles when he got home from work. He went from weighing 230 pounds to being sober and healthy at 149 pounds. It also helped him to sleep at night.

Eminem recently posted a picture on his Instagram to his millions of followers. The picture was of a medallion he received from alcoholics anonymous. It read "To Thine Own Self Be True, Unity, Service, Recovery." In the middle of the medallion there was a roman numeral XI, for 11 years being sober.[39] He remains sober to this day.

Grant Cardone

Grant Cardone is a serial bestselling author, CEO of Cardone Capital, real estate tycoon, father of two, and husband to Elena Cardone. He is also the founder of the 10X Movement and The 10x Growth Conference. He has spoken at the Pentagon and he holds the most successful entrepreneur and business conference in the world. He also founded the Cardone Foundation, with the philosophy "Let's teach success to those who think it's out of reach."[40]

When Cardone was 10 his father died and his mother was left to raise five kids on her own, as a single mother. The pain of losing his father led him to becoming angry at life as well as at

---

[39] Katie Scott, "Eminem celebrates 10 years of sobriety," *Global News*, April 24, 2018. https://globalnews.ca/news/4164423/eminem-sober/

[40] Grant Cardone, "What Is Grant Cardone Foundation," Grant Cardone Foundation, accessed June 6, 2020. https://cardonefoundation.com/

himself. At 16, he was introduced to drugs and alcohol, and within one year, he was doing every drug there was.

Grant Cardone was an addict. He tried to quit drugs and alcohol ten times a day, for nine years.[41] But, as he says, if you get into alcohol and drugs, you will hang out with similar people. Cardone overdosed three times when he was 25. His mom finally told him to leave and he decided to commit himself to rehab for 28 days. Without that, he believes, he would have died.

Grant was able to successfully recover and inspire millions of people across the world to give up drugs and alcohol and focus on their purpose. He now says that drugs and alcohol is a waste of time and leads to poor decisions and poverty.[42]

I am very grateful for everything that Grant Cardone has done for me, including teaching me about business and his leadership by example. He influenced me to give up drugs and alcohol; now I am doing what he asked everyone else to do: pay it forward. Because, as he says, "That's what multiplies the power and the strength for recovery."

"Quit getting wasted, quit wasting weekends, quit wasting time, and figure out what you can get great at and give back," Cardone says. "We're unstoppable."[43]

---

[41] Rob Moore, *'I Overdosed 3 Times' Grant Cardone Opens up About Drug Addiction*, YouTube video, December 21, 2019. https://www.youtube.com/watch?v=Tj59P0h9qPA

[42] Evan Carmichael, *Another Grant Cardone Top 10 Rules For Success*, YouTube video, August 3, 2018. https://www.youtube.com/watch?v=OKDlMViICPY

[43] Grant Cardone, *How to Turnaround Your Life*, YouTube video, July 2, 2017. https://www.youtube.com/watch?v=YGwxRopBxmA

Bill Wilson was born in a room behind a bar in his grandparents' hotel in East Dorset, Vermont, on Thanksgiving, in the middle of a snowstorm, on November 26, 1895. Bill had a happy childhood, until his parents abandoned him.[44]

When Bill was 11, his parents divorced. His father left for British Columbia to take a job as a quarryman. His mother departed to Boston, where she was one of the first women to receive a degree from Harvard University in osteopathic medicine. Bill and his sister Dorothy, who was four years younger than him, were raised by his mother's grandparents, Fayette and Ella Griffith, in a tiny house in New England, without their parents. This was very painful for Bill, as you can imagine.[45]

Bill Wilson met Lois Burnham, the sister of a friend, in 1913. They fell in love and became inseparable; they get engaged in secret in 1915, and they were married on January 24, 1918, just before Wilson went off to fight in the first world war in Europe.

But another life change had also already taken place for him. When he was 21 years old, in 1917, he was at a party in Massachusetts, and he had his first alcoholic drink. "Lo, the

---

[44] Editorial Staff, "Bill Wilson," *Alcoholrehab.com*, October 9, 2020. https://alcoholrehab.com/alcoholism/bill-wilson/

[45] "Bill's Story," Stepping Stones, accessed June 22, 2020. https://www.steppingstones.org/billsstory.html

miracle!" he later wrote. "I belonged to the universe; I was a part of things at last. . . . I had found the elixir of life."[46] [47]

He had found his escape from pain, and reality. He got really drunk that night, and he ended up vomiting and passing out. He became a problem drinker from his very first drink of alcohol. He never could have guessed that one drink would lead him to becoming a hopeless alcoholic and send him on a downward spiral that would cost him his career and health, and contribute to him destroying his finances, while almost costing him his life—all at the same time.[48]

When Bill returned from the war, he wanted to start a family with Lois. The couple had a series of failed ectopic pregnancies, and they found they were unable to bear children. They tried to adopt but were denied—agencies did background checks and would not allow them to adopt because of Bill's drinking, which had continued to increase heavily.[49]

---

[46] "Bill's Story," Stepping Stones, accessed June 22, 2020.
https://www.steppingstones.org/billsstory.html

[47] Susan Cheever, "The Healer: Bill Wilson," *Time*, reproduced at Rewritables.net, accessed June 22, 2020.
http://www.rewritables.net/cybriety/time_magazine_article_about_bill_wilson.h
tm

[48] "Bill's Story," Stepping Stones, accessed June 22, 2020.
https://www.steppingstones.org/billsstory.html; Susan Cheever, "The Healer: Bill Wilson," *Time*, reproduced at Rewritables.net, accessed June 22, 2020. http://www.rewritables.net/cybriety/time_magazine_article_about_bill_wilson.h
tm

[49] "Lois' Story," Stepping Stones, accessed June 22, 2020.
https://www.steppingstones.org/loisstory.html

He worked on Wall Street during the 1920s, and when he had success he would drink, and when he lost money he would also drink. "I was drinking to dream greater dreams of power, dreams of domination. Money was to me never a symbol of security, it was a symbol of prestige and power," he wrote.[50]

Then in 1929, when the stock market crashed, he lost his job on Wall Street and went $60,000 in debt.[51] He drank even more. "I began to turn violent and talk such gibberish that people about me were frightened to death," he recalled.[52]

Wilson's drinking had gotten so out of control that Lois tried to lock him into their house to stop him from drinking. But she was unsuccessful, because he hid bottles of liquor at their house and drank alone while she was at work.[53]

Wilson would drink until he would have total blackouts, followed by horrific hangovers. Alcohol was an uncontrollable addiction for him. He could not stop himself from drinking for more than a short while at a time and he was told by doctors that he would most likely die if he did not stop drinking.

And then he had an experience that changed his life forever.

At the time, there was a herbal remedy called the Belladonna Cure that supposedly cured 9 out of 10 alcoholics. Wilson, however, was turning out to be the tenth. He had been to the

---

[50] Don Lattin, *Distilled Spirits*, University of California Press, 2012.

[51] Bob Frost, "A Man With Friends: Bill Wilson ('Bill W.')," *Biography*, 2002. http://www.historyaccess.com/billwilson-hista.html

[52] Don Lattin, *Distilled Spirits*, University of California Press, 2012.

[53] Don Lattin, *Distilled Spirits*, University of California Press, 2012.

hospital three times, and before his fourth visit, he went to a grocery store, got four beers, and drank them on his way to the hospital. He was finishing the fourth one as he walked in.

Wilson had been in the hospital for several days when "suddenly, my room blazed with an indescribably white light. I was seized with an ecstasy beyond description. Every joy I had known was pale by comparison. . . . Then, seen in the mind's eye, there was a mountain. I stood upon its summit where a great wind blew. A wind, not of air, but of spirit. In great, clean strength it blew right through me. Then came the blazing thought, 'You are a free man.'"[54]

Bill Wilson never drank again. On December 18, 1934, he was released from hospital, and he was determined to make a positive impact in the world.

After his spiritual revelation, Bill Wilson had a meeting with an Ohio surgeon named Dr. Robert Smith. The meeting was supposed to last only 15 minutes, but ended up going on for hours. They were talking about how an alcoholic can help another alcoholic. "Because of our kinship in suffering," Bill wrote, "our channels of contact have always been charged with the language of the heart."

A month later, on June 10, 1935, Wilson and Smith started what would become Alcoholics Anonymous. Bill wrote a book soon after on his principles for recovering from alcohol addiction and their way to sobriety. The book was condensed down to

---

[54] Don Lattin, *Distilled Spirits*, University of California Press, 2012.

400 pages, and was finally titled *Alcoholics Anonymous*. It gave its name to the foundation.[55]

What Bill Wilson did, with his principles of social support, accountability, and honesty, has helped millions of people recover from alcoholism.[56]

---

[55] Susan Cheever, "The Healer: Bill Wilson," *Time*, reproduced at Rewritables.net, accessed June 22, 2020.
http://www.rewritables.net/cybriety/time_magazine_article_about_bill_wilson.htm

[56] Jennifer Bleyer, "A Radical New Approach to Beating Addiction," *Psychology Today*, June 14, 2019.
https://www.psychologytoday.com/ca/articles/201705/radical-new-approach-beating-addiction

AND ME

My last alcoholic drink was in February, 2020. As I'm writing this in October 2020, I've now realized the importance of mindset and how dependent I previously was on alcohol for temporary happiness and confidence. I would just go out and get blackout drunk—I would start conversations and hardly remember what was going on. Then I would be hung over and unproductive the next day, until night, when I would go out to the liquor store, buy more alcohol, and party again. I know many people who are stuck in this cycle and it leads nowhere.

Alcohol cost me money, it cost me opportunities, it cost me experiences. It could have cost me my life.

Do You Want to Live Forever?

Ray Kurzweil, the American author and inventor and animal rights activist, wrote in his great book *Fantastic Voyage: Live Long Enough to Live Forever* about the dangers of consuming alcohol:

> Say someone drinks a small amount of alcohol. This increases the release of pleasurable neurotransmitters such as dopamine in the brain. Excessive consumption,

however, depletes the brain's supply of dopamine as well as several other neurotransmitters associated with feelings of well-being and pleasure. In an attempt to feel better, alcoholics drink more and more, further depleting levels of these neurotransmitters and creating an uncontrolled downward spiral.[57]

In another great book, *The Singularity Is Near*, Kurzweil lists and explains radical life-extending technologies that will become available in the future and will increase our life expectancy and potentially enable us to live forever. These technologies include cell therapies and gene chips; their potentials include reversing degenerative diseases, combating heart disease, preventing DNA mutations, overcoming cancer, and reversing aging.[58]

I highly recommend Kurzweil's books.

We know that alcohol is very addictive, is bad for your body and can even cause cancer, is a gateway drug, and leads to bad decisions—which could lead to early death.

Why risk it, when there is a possibility to live forever if we can stay healthy and live long enough?

---

[57] Ray Kurzweil and Terry Grossman, *Fantastic Voyage: Live Long Enough to Live Forever*, Penguin, 2005.

[58] Ray Kurzweil, *The Singularity Is Near*, Viking, 2005.

WHAT CAN YOU DO?

When you decide to be sober, do it for yourself. You don't have to have any approval from anyone else. You must fire the people from your life who are toxic, because they will do everything they can to hold you down with them.

If someone wants to put a class one carcinogen inside of their body and drink a diluted poison, that's their problem, not yours.

Gratitude and keeping busy helps to recover from alcohol addiction. It is also good to sign up for Alcoholics Anonymous and join local support groups of people who have alcohol addictions.

Be involved in social activities. Comedy shows, yoga, sports teams, activism and protests— all are great social activities where you can be sober and connect with people. There are also "sober bars" popping up across the world that are good to go to and meet people.

I was able to overcome being an alcoholic by realizing that I was an alcoholic and by doing things to serve others. I became a human and animal rights activist and co-founded the Light Movement, which gave me fulfillment. I began learning French, I wrote *The Christian Bubble* and *Compassion Is Not a*

Crime, I read books, I took business courses, I joined a gym, I started taking Brazilian Jiu Jitsu and Karate… all activities that kept me busy and my mind off of alcohol. I have been ten times as productive since I quit drinking.

Stay limitless, drug and alcohol free, and together, let's make the world a better place.

With love and gratitude.

Kyle Ferguson

CAN YOU DO ME A FAVOR?

Thanks for reading "Why I Stopped Drinking". Would you please write a review about this book on Amazon? I would greatly appreciate it! Reviews are a great way to spread awareness and build momentum and help make the world a better place. Click here to leave a review on Amazon.com Note: If the link does not work on your device, please visit Amazon manually and navigate to "Why I Stopped Drinking", and leave a review. Thank you – I really appreciate your support!

ACKNOWLEDGEMENTS

I am grateful for the miracle of life and I am incredibly grateful that I was born in Canada. Being born as a Canadian gave me the freedom and opportunity to travel the world, which opened my mind and gave me perspective. Thank you to my parents, Scott and Karen, for allowing me to pursue my dreams in life.

Thank you, Mark Cuban, for teaching me that time is the most precious asset and you should be doing what is most important with time. Your life lesson made me realize that it was an absolute must to complete this book.

Thank you, James Harbeck, for being a great editor. You did a great job of giving this book structure, flow, and power.

Thank you, Derek Young, for being an amazing friend and giving me a Kindle, which led me to read and write relentlessly. Thank you, Tim Keck, for being a great friend and providing wisdom and encouragement for me to write this book. Thank you Riley Keck for your great personality and thank you for inspiring me to dedicate my life to being a voice for the voiceless.

Thank you, Chris McGinn, for being a great friend and thank

you for your indefatigable, utterly relentless dedication to human and animal rights activism on the Light Movement.

Thank you, Peter Buffett, for helping me find my path to fulfillment and opening my mind with your wonderful book: Life is What You Make it: Find Your Own Path to Fulfillment.

Thank you, Jeff Bezos, for creating Amazon Kindle, and thank you for providing the opportunity to publish this book on your website. And thank you for being a great leader and teaching me to be relentless.

Thank you, Nikola Tesla and Swami Vivekananda, for teaching me to do my best to make the world a better place each and every day.

Thank you, Charlie Tian, for giving me the chance to write for GuruFocus, which gave me the opportunity to practice writing and the importance of momentum.

Thank you Nick and Tom Karadza for teaching me the importance of having an abundance mindset and building and maintaining momentum in life.

Thank you JT Foxx for teaching me to be relentless and thank you for leading by example and not drinking. Thank you for also teaching me that 70% of my time should be spent building relationships, and thank you for teaching me to think practice!

Thank you Grant Cardone for teaching me to set goals and follow through with them.

Thank you Kyle Maynard for teaching me that there are no excuses in life and that you must be willing to do whatever it takes to get what you want.

Thank you Daymond John and Bob Proctor for teaching me the importance of focus and mind set.

Thank you Leslie Dixon for writing Limitless. And thank you to the entire cast of Limitless for doing a great job in the movie. Limitless helped me expand my consciousness. Limitless is my favourite movie, and I watched it countless times as I completed this book. I am forever grateful.

Thank you to all the motivational speakers and people who I have had the opportunity to listen to and keep me motivated as I faced adversity and hurdled obstacle after obstacle.

Thank you to all of the people who have been a positive influence on my life, I am forever grateful, and I love you all!